Contents

Introduction

If we can learn to heal ourselves then we will have the time to learn to love what is around us; if we can learn to love what is around us, then we can learn to heal the world.

If you already have some understanding of Reiki, you will know that the common belief is that you must be 'attuned' to receive Reiki energy by a Master before you can embark on your healing journey.

However, there are a great number of people who have woken up to the fact that the universal energy is within the reach of every one of us. We are all born the same, holding the same energies within us, and all we are trying to do is find our way. With the use of Self-Healing Reiki we can all turn the corner from trying to find our way, to making it our way.

What is Reiki?

Reiki is a form of healing administered through touch and the use of symbols, promoting the body's healing process on an emotional, mental, physical and spiritual level. Reiki is very similar to spiritual healing where energy enters the body through the crown chakra and is emitted from the palms, reducing stress and aiding relaxation and bringing balance to our lives.

The word Reiki is made up of two Japanese words: *Rei* meaning universal power or spirit and *Ki* meaning life force or energy. Reiki is often known as 'Universal life force energy'. The ki is very similar to the chi used in Chinese acupuncture and Tai Chi, the graceful movement that uses exercises and breathing to flow energy through the body.

All living things are made up of energy and it is this energy that sustains life; without the body's energy there is no physical form of us.

Everyone has the ability to learn to use Reiki, from a child to the elderly. Reiki is always safe to use regardless of anyone's condition. It is like the unconditional love of a mother when she cuddles and comforts her sick or hurt child, bringing her child the warmth of love and energy. We have all given ourselves and others healing without knowing it one way or another. Think of the times you have rested your head within your palms to soothe the pain of a headache, or the stomach pain your hands have rubbed away.

It is an excellent complementary therapy to use alongside any other form of healing, conventional or alternative, and frequently produces beneficial results. Reiki is an intelligent energy, it will know where healing is needed first.

The History of Reiki

Reiki is a Tibetan form of healing said to have been rediscovered by a man called Dr Mikao Usui, who spent many years looking for the greater purpose of life. After some time he came to the conclusion that the ultimate purpose was to be in a complete state of peace within the mind. To achieve this he asked for guidance from a Zen master, hopeful of being told how to achieve a state of peace within the mind, but he did not get the response that he was hoping for.

'If it is enlightenment that you seek and you feel the need to know the purpose of life then I suggest you die,' said the Zen master.

This disheartened Usui and he found himself at a loss as to what to do next; he felt his life would be over if he couldn't find an answer to this question.

Usui's 21-day Meditational Journey

In despair, Dr Usui climbed to the top of Mount Kuri Yama, where he collected 21 stones to serve as a calendar for a 21-day meditation and fast, and at the end of each day he threw away one stone. On the 21st day, with the last stone in his hand, he prayed that he would find the answers he was looking for. But, still none the wiser at the end of the day, he prepared to find the answers in death.

Just as Dr Usui was about to jump from the

mountain's edge, a beam of light hurtled towards him, knocking him from his feet and bringing him an overwhelming feeling of peace. The light was made up of millions of small dazzling lights, some changing in colour and moving together to form shapes and symbols. Each one had a meaning and purpose, and spiritual and healing properties to activate healing energies.

Weak from the meditation but excited to share his discovery with the Zen master, Usui stumbled down the mountain. On his descent he stubbed his toe, and, comforting the pain with his hands, he was amazed to see his injury healing before his eyes.

When he reached the bottom of the mountain he found a place to eat and tucked into a traditional Japanese meal. The innkeeper, knowing about his meditation and fast, advised him not to eat such a large amount, as it would be dangerous after such a long time without food. But to his surprise, Usui did not get any stomach pains. When Usui told the innkeeper about his discovery and how he had healed himself, the innkeeper asked if he could heal his granddaughter's toothache. This Usui did by putting his hands on her jaw.

On returning to the Zen master he found him bedridden with sickness; using his new knowledge he placed his hands over the Zen master, bringing him back to health with great success.

Reiki Symbols

For a long time Reiki symbols were kept secret, and were shown only to those who had been attuned to the second degree of Reiki. Many masters wouldn't even let their students keep any drawn copies and insisted they were destroyed after training.

Used as a directional tool these symbols can best be explained as keys that open the doors to Reiki energy for self-healing of the past, present and future. We can use symbols over a wide range, as you will come to understand, not only on ourselves but also on the objects around us. They give us the means to connect with specific frequencies, and using different symbols will boost the Reiki energy. You can use the Reiki energy with the symbols by drawing the symbol in the air with your finger or using your mind to imagine you are doing so, then saying the name of the symbol three times.

Sei Hei ki

The mental and emotional symbol pronounced 'say-hay-key'. Helpful for healing relationship problems, emotional or mental stress, depression, anger, sadness, it also enhances the memory (as connected to the subconscious mind). This is considered an uplifting symbol because of the way this energy leaves one with feelings of emotional balance within the mind.

To clear a room of any negativity, stand facing each corner and use your finger to draw the symbol in the air around the corners of the room; you can also use incense sticks in the same way. Practise by placing your finger on the top point of the left character following round in one flowing movement. Then do the same for the right character, top to bottom then follow over the two curves. Draw once and say the name three times.

Cho Ku Rei

The power symbol, pronounced 'choh-koo-ray', also increases the energy of Reiki. Start a self-healing treatment by drawing Cho Ku Rei on your palms. Visualize Cho Ku Rei around your loved ones to keep them safe. Cho Ku Rei every doorway of your home to keep a strong positive energy around. Reiki your food before you eat it, your bath water for an energy enriched bath, even your journey before you begin it. When drawing start at the top point and follow round in one flowing movement.

Fifteen-year-old Robert tells how Reiki symbols helped him when he was being bullied. 'I drew Cho Ku Rei, the power symbol to bring confidence, on a piece of card and on the other side I drew Sei Hei Ki to keep negativity away. I kept the card with me all the time, and soon the bully left me alone and I had more self-confidence.'

Hon Sha Ze Sho Nen

Pronounced 'hone-sha-zay-show-nen', this is the distance healing symbol, known for sending Reiki healing energies over time and space (past, present and future) to anyone and anything. Seen as a sending energy, but also a receiver when drawn and kept on your body, clothing or even under your pillow when you sleep. Hon Sha Ze Sho Nen is the most complex of the three symbols, so use this book to familiarize yourself with it.

Seventy-one-year-old Joan explains how she broke a bone in her foot. To aid the healing, she drew the Hon Sha Ze Sho Nen on her foot. When she went to the hospital a week later, her doctor was amazed that her foot was healing so quickly and that she was already able to walk unaided. 'That's Reiki for you,' Joan explained.

The Aura and Chakras

We all have an aura; it is an energy field of several layers and colours that surrounds every living thing. The colours within the aura change along with our moods and thoughts. The layer closest to the physical form is called the etheric; this is the densest layer, and therefore the easiest to feel and see.

Chakras

Chakras are spinning vortexes of energy found within the aura. The chakras balance life between body and spirit. Chakra is an ancient Indian word meaning 'wheel'. The traditional Hindu culture system names seven main chakras within the human energy system, from the coccyx to the crown, although there are many more, one being in the palms of the hands. They are traditionally depicted as a lotus flower moving at different frequencies and with different colours.

Reiki Self-Attunement

Sit in a quiet, comfortable space and concentrate on your breathing. As you breathe in know that you are breathing in energy from around you, as you breathe out know that you are holding this energy within you. Let it be known to the universe that you wish to receive Reiki by saying, 'I ask the Reiki energy to be brought to me for my mind, body and soul so that I may use it for healing on all levels of my life.' Within your mind's eye see your crown chakra as a lotus flower with its petals opening. When the flower is fully open the Reiki energy can flow through you by entering the crown chakra.

Healing the Body

Before you begin ask the universe to bring Reiki to you for healing of mind, body and soul. As with attunement, draw this energy through your crown chakra to blend with your body's energy. Using your finger, draw the Cho Ku Rei symbol on both palms. This combined energy will flow from your hands to wherever you position them on the body. A full session could take thirty to fifty minutes. Hold hand positions for three to five minutes, then move to the next.

Position 1: The Head

Let your mind and body relax; now place both hands at the top of the head slightly to the back, palms touching the head. This is a very calming meditative position as it represents the first touch we receive at birth.

Position 2: The Eyes

Throughout the day your eyes take thousands of pictures and are continually focusing on all that you see.

Close your eyes and with your hands keeping a gentle touch on your body at all times, slowly slide your palms forward over the top of your head so they come to rest over the eyes. You may feel some heat or tingling within the palms of your hands.

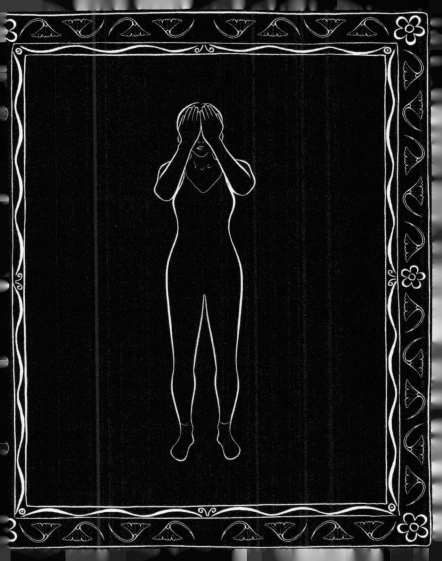

Position 3: The Ears

Some of the sounds we hear aren't as beautiful as the morning song of the birds, and for some, like tinnitus sufferers, peaceful moments are difficult to come by.

Gently slide both your hands backwards so that your palms are resting over your ears. As you make this movement let the tips of your fingers brush away any stress from your forehead.

Position 4:
The Jaw and Mouth

The mouth and jaw play an important role in our daily lives; your smile is often the first thing people notice about you. The tongue and lips help us to form words and our jaw and teeth make up our chewing action. When you have pain in this area, the last thing you feel like doing is smiling.

With a downward and forward movement slide your palms from the ears to the jaw line. Cup your jaw between your palms, gently drop your head forward and let the hands support the weight of your head. Throughout any healing session you may feel different sensations within the palms, but if you don't, don't be disheartened, Reiki is still being received.

Position 5:
The Neck and Shoulders

The neck is the support structure for the head and protects the spinal cord. The brain's messages and major blood vessels travel through the neck to the body. We all have times of tension within the neck, and one of the most common injuries we suffer is whiplash and limited rotation. The neck gives us the ability to hold our head up high with confidence, but also to drop our head down and hide in the shadows.

So now, with confidence, hold your head up high and move your palms around your neck and above the shoulders. When you feel you've found an area that needs attention hold your palms there.

Position 6: The Heart

The heart is the body's centre of love; all life's experiences have an effect on the heart. Our emotions are heart felt: joy, happiness and love as well as the painful emotions of sorrow, sadness and fear which can have a damaging effect on the heart. We have all heard the saying 'she died of a broken heart'. So the heart may be the strongest and hardest-working muscle, working non-stop to pump blood and oxygen around the body, but it can also be the weakest.

Place both hands over the heart and connect with this centre of love, feeling Reiki bringing the healing energy of love to every heartbeat.

Position 7: The Lungs

The lungs perform many functions, breathing being the most essential; in addition, they play an important part in the body's defence against infection. With each breath the lungs take in oxygen and remove carbon dioxide. When we are in a relaxed state of mind we take longer, calmer breaths, making life feel calm, quiet and relaxed. When we put ourselves under stress we make our lungs work twice as hard by taking shorter but harder breaths.

Rest your palms in line with the lungs and as you inhale, breathe in positive energy feeling the warmth of healing within you. As you exhale, breathe out any negative energy within you.

There isn't any set time with healing, so when the time feels right move to the next position.

Position 8: The Liver, Spleen and Pancreas

These organs, especially the liver, remove toxins from the body. The pancreas produces chemicals that are crucial to the digestive process. By applying healing to these organs, Reiki stimulates the body's immune system.

If you place your right hand over the area under the ribs on the right side of your body your palm will just about cover the area of the liver. Place your left hand on the upper left side of your abdomen for the spleen and pancreas.

Position 9: The Stomach

The stomach is part of the digestive system. Stomach ailments are often associated with the third chakra which is located in the solar plexus. If we ever feel uncomfortable in the presence of someone else we tend to cross our arms over the solar plexus.

Position your hands one above the other, one on the upper abdomen and the other on the lower abdomen.

Position 10:
The Pelvic Area

The pelvis supports the weight of your upper body and is commonly known as the hip bone. The main organs within this area are the bladder, prostate, rectum and reproductive system.

1 Place your palms in a V shape above the groin on the pelvic area for healing the reproductive organs, bladder and for soothing period pains.

2 Slide both hands to your sides for healing the hip joint.

3 Move your hands round to your lower back forming the V shape with your fingers over the coccyx.

Reiki can also be used throughout pregnancy to give healing to you and your unborn baby.

1   2   3

Position 11: Upper Leg
Position 12: Lower Leg

Our legs take us everywhere we need to go, but it's not until we come across a health problem that we realize how much we take them for granted.

1 Using the sense of touch, guide your hands over your legs by placing a palm on each of your thighs.

2 Gently slide your palms to rest over the knee caps.

3 Gradually work towards the lower part of the legs including the calf muscles.

4 Continue sliding down until your hands rest on your ankles.

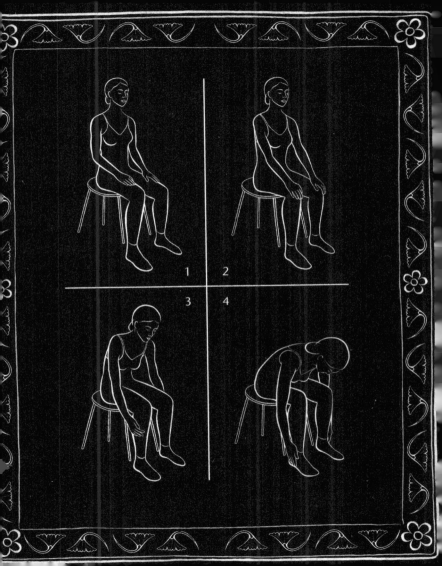

1 2

3 4

Position 13: The Feet

Healing the entire body can be achieved just through healing the feet. The feet are the support of the whole body; our standing place on the Earth, every footstep guiding us through the journey of life. Just as Usui did with his first healing experience, clasp both hands around each foot and with the same trust and belief in Reiki as Usui had, know that Reiki is and always will be there for you.

You don't have to be in ill health to give yourself Reiki, just think of it as an uplifting tonic keeping you in tip top condition.

The Heart's Energy Expanding the Aura

After you have performed your self-healing exercises, you can expand the healing energy to your aura, using the heart's energy of love.

1 Stand with your feet apart and your hands by your sides.

2 On your inward breath bring your palms to your heart chakra, focusing on the energy of love.

3 On your outward breath see the heart's energy of love within your palms and raise your hands above your head.

4 With arms stretched push your palms outwards, expanding the aura with love, then bring your hands back to your sides.

Complete the exercise three times.

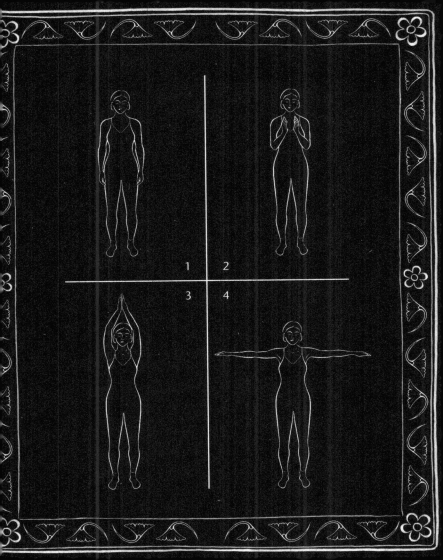

1 2

3 4

The Three
Energies Meditation

Universal, Body and Earth

Using the Earth and the Universal energies will help you to bring balance to your life. Close your eyes; hear and feel every breath that you take. As you breathe in, you breathe air that energizes you, as you breathe out you hold this energy within you. Imagine the soles of your feet as a sponge soaking up the earth's energy; with every breath you take this energy is combining with your energy. Now visualize your crown chakra as a lotus flower with petals open, receiving Reiki. To help bring a balanced state within mind, body and soul imagine the energies as different colours blending into one. When you feel ready move your toes and fingers to sense a connection back with your normal waking consciousness.

This meditation can be performed daily.

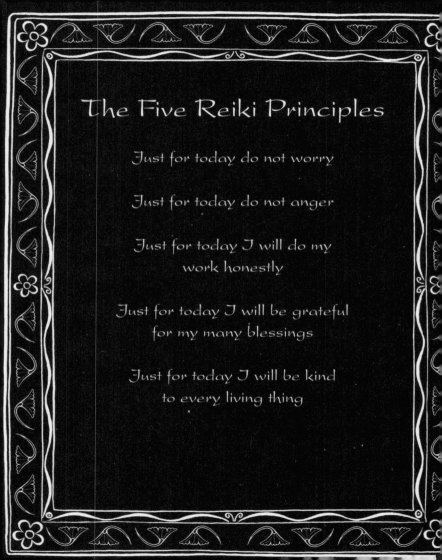

The Five Reiki Principles

Just for today do not worry

Just for today do not anger

Just for today I will do my
work honestly

Just for today I will be grateful
for my many blessings

Just for today I will be kind
to every living thing

The five Reiki principles are about taking responsibility for who you are and being aware of what impact your actions make on your life and the world around you. Just think about it; if you could put the five principles into practice every day, how much more relaxed, calm, focused, centred and fulfilled you would become.

When we worry we push every good thought away from us.

When you rise above your moments of anger you feel a change within your body, bringing peace into the mind and clarity of thought.

By supporting yourself honestly, you do not harbour negative feelings.

Showing gratitude for your blessings brings joy to your mind, body and soul.

Being kind to every living thing, you hold humanity within your heart.

Every day say the principles to yourself and make them part of your day.

Healing the Mind

The mind is one place you can truly call your own. You could lay every part of your physical body out on a table and say this is me, but you cannot put your thoughts, memories, emotions, perception, will or imagination out for all to see. Before you can heal your mind, for instance, from stress, anxiety or depression you need to believe in yourself, feel confident and even begin to like yourself.

To begin to heal your mind: use the Sei Hei Ki symbol (page 13) for healing on an emotional level, for bringing peace and harmony. Then take some time to read over and familiarize yourself with the five Reiki principles (page 50). Lastly, use the heart's self-healing position (page 32) to bring healing to your heart: a healthy heart means a happy mind.

Sending Healing
to the Past

Sometimes things that happen in our past affect the way we feel at this present moment and steer our future to a different direction than the one that was planned for us. To get yourself back on track ask for the Reiki energy to be brought to you so you can send healing to the past to help your future.

Visualize the Reiki symbol Hon Sha Ze Sho Nen (see page 17) in front of you and as you breathe in, feel the energy of the symbol entering you. Think of the time and place you want to heal, see and feel it in the way you want it to be, ask the Reiki energies to be sent to that time and place, then watch the symbol leaving your body, travelling to heal your future journey.

Reiki Shower Exercise

This is a great way to start your day. As you step out of bed let it be known to the universe that you wish to receive the Reiki energy. Close your eyes and in your mind see this energy as drops of rain falling from the sky, encasing you. Feel this energy absorbing through the pores of your skin, running through all your muscles and internal organs, setting you up for the day.

If you decide to do the exercise when taking a shower the procedure is the same, just with the added bonus of the warmth of the water.

Walking into the Cho Ku Rei Energy

Sometimes we need a little extra help from Reiki — for example for an exam, or a job interview, or the first day of work. Any stressful or difficult situation can become a little easier to get through with the help of the Cho Ku Rei energy.

With your mind or hand draw the Cho Ku Rei symbol. Visualize and believe that this symbol is floating in front of you; a dazzling light of pure energy, as Dr Usui might have seen on Mount Kuri Yama. Now walk forward so you're standing within the symbol, absorbing the power and energy of Cho Ku Rei.

If you are unable to walk through, use your mind to bring the symbol to you.

Brushing away the Day's Attachments Exercise

Sometimes at the end of the day, just as you intend to go to sleep, the last thing you want on your mind is that day's events. We all pick up things through the day physically, emotionally and even in our aura, and over time these could lead to illness, blockages and emotional problems. So, at the end of each day ask the universe to bring the Reiki energy to you, state your intent and visualize the energy entering your body through the crown chakra combining with your body's own energies.

Starting at the top of your head using your palms, slowly brush down the whole of your body, brushing away everything that isn't needed. This should leave you feeling calm and relaxed, ready for a good night's sleep.

Grounding

When self-healing or meditating, if you ever find yourself feeling light of body or perhaps feeling as if your feet are not firmly on the ground, you may need to perform the grounding exercise. This will help to bring you back to being centred within your body.

Visualize roots sprouting from the soles of your feet and working their way into the ground, anchoring you to the earth beneath.

The Soul's Energy

The aura that encircles your entire body is your soul's energy, the heart within you is the soul's seed planted to grow: the connection between body and soul.

By being able to feel this energy it will bring you a deeper understanding of some of the energies that life has to show us, if we choose to look for them, Reiki being one of them.

To feel this energy first rub your hands together, then hold your palms out in front of you, shoulder-width apart. Slowly bring them together, and as they become closer gently bounce the energy back and forth. With practice you will begin to feel a ball of energy between your palms.

The Reiki
Plant Exercise

This is a fun exercise to do and a great way for you to see what a good impact Reiki can have on the world by just starting with a small plant, because as we all know, from small things great things grow.

Find two plants of the same type and size. On one pot draw the Cho Ku Rei symbol; this is the plant you are going to give Reiki to. Place them both on a window sill where they will get the same amount of light, and water when required. Once a day ask for the Reiki energy to be brought to you so you may give healing to the plant with the symbol. Without touching the plant start with your hands around the pot to heal the roots, then move up and around the plant. Over time you should see that the plant receiving healing is growing quicker than the other.

Acknowledgements

To Pat Gardener for opening my mind to the knowledge of healing hands.

To Susan Swain for guiding my path to Reiki.

To Leonora van Gils for the first steps along the path of Reiki.

To my wife Sharon for her love and support.

To Martin Faulks for seeing the dream.

I would also like to thank Watkins Publishing for bringing Reiki to you.

Dedicated to Peter John Cook, thank you for the happy times you brought. I know you shine a light over us all and as you would say; Happy days, Dad, love Brian.